DEW DROPS FROM HEAVEN

Quotes

By Todd L Thomas

Editor Priscilla Chana

Presented by:

Streams Of Mercy Ministries

Dedicated to the Memory

Of

Lillie A. Thomas

Special Thanks:

Andy Anding III, Ron G. Scott and James Wood

Thank you Pastor Bill Johnson and Bethel Church for pouring into me, so that I can pour out Christ to others.

Lord please bless my children, grandchildren and generations to come. Lord, touch their lives in a great and mighty.

-TLT

Published by Streams Of Mercy Ministries

Copyright 2014 Streams Of Mercy, ASCAP

Bless you Clive
with the love of
the Lord
Yeshua Ha-Mashiach

[signature]

QUOTES

PLEASE CHECK IN YOUR RELIGION HERE before proceeding any further into this book. I will not be responsible for what happens to your religion beyond this point, if you do not... lol. If you are not religious, WOO HOO

Someone please call 9-1-1... Apparently I've been infected with a deeper, non-religious relationship with God. I don't think there is a cure. At least I hope not.

This world has nothing for us. But as believers, we have all the world will ever want and need... and we can't wait to give it to them... it's fun... it's addicting... it's contagious... it's love... our very source of life... our destiny realized...

It's easier to put money in the offering plate to pay the surrogate house evangelist or minister to win souls for Christ on our behalf... then it is to have Jesus living inside of us, and releasing heaven into the lives of others, fulfilling our Great Commission. One takes our money. The other requires our lives. But only one brings joy unspeakable, as we fulfil our call.

Intimate relationship and fellowship between creation (us) and Creator (God) is true Kingdom Culture Life defined.

To be deeply in love with God is to align ourselves with His righteousness, His holiness, His goodness, His character, His values... because we don't want to fall and re-defile the Lover of our soul to the cross. There is a matter of discipline with Daddy God as well. This is the reverential fear of God at work, where the carnal mind has no place to dwell in us... where our relationship with the Son, the Bridegroom, is our passion... and His Love is our one true desire... so we take upon our lives the mind of Christ where His life is now living in us.

We've got to get over ourselves and get Jesus...

I am a Lover of Jesus. I'm anything but ashamed to say it. In fact, I openly declare it from the rooftops and in the marketplace. What am I to be ashamed of?... that I'm in love with the One who saved my soul from the grasp of the enemy of God and man? ...from the enemy of my very soul? ...from the one who wants to drag me to his pit with him for eternity? Hey, I'm breaking out my dancing shoes. Are you kidding me? I want to dance with the lover of my soul.

Hear the cry of your Bride's heart... pour out to us Your precious Holy Spirit to lead and guide us... to reveal the Father heart of God. I pray we could truly understand the rhythm and harmony of Your Love... that the song we sing out from the mountaintops and even the valleys would draw the lost. Anoint us to win souls that are sold out to Jesus and only Jesus... souls that win souls... yes, we are Your children, Lord... and we share in the joy of the work of the harvest fields...

When we can learn from the experiences of others, we can learn to avoid the pitfalls they encountered, and move even further than the forerunners and pioneers... we can stand on their shoulders and continue the race, the good fight, in our pursuit of a deeper intimacy with God for us to share with others.

We encounter trials as aliens of this world. Now I am a citizen of heaven. I am told by God to take dominion of the earth. And He made me a warrior... armed and dangerous with the Word of God and the Armour of Light. I am equipped. I am ready. And no fiery dart of the enemy shall stop me. Nothing of this world can withstand my God who goes before me. What shall I fear?

How can I but sit at His feet and love Him? I understand fully, that in the midst of my fallen human condition, the God of this universe reached down to earth, plucked me from the hands of the enemy and placed me on the Glory Train headed for eternity. He loved me before the foundations of the world and He loves me now, with Christ living in and through me. He has pursued my heart just as I pursue Him now.

I walked in the shadows, I walked in religiosity... and everything in-between. And there He was, arms open wide to me, the King of Gory... the One who pursued me... the One who has shown me He is more than real, and deeply in love with me. He has shown me His Power, His Mercy, His Grace, His Love. How can I be anything but smitten for His unfailing, undying Love? I have no desire to live the life of Todd anymore, but to lay that life down, take up my cross and follow my Lover, Jesus... to have Him pour in and through me. His very heart beats in me. I pour out like a fountain, the life of the One... the Christ... Jesus... THIS is life worth living. THIS is life worth every new day mission. THIS is life worth dying for. THIS is life worth believing for. THIS is my spiritual journey.

Kingdom Culture Living is a life with Christ by your side at all times... being mentored by the Spirit of the Living God... being so lost in the Him, You and He are One... like husband and wife, rich and intimate... it is an "others - centred life", walking in the authority of heaven, touching souls with a deposit of God, that they too might know the Kingdom life.

In your spiritual journey as you walk out your commissioned life, know that you will meet resistance. Also know the Blood of Jesus goes before you in battle. If you're not at war, you might want to find out why the enemy is not opposed to you. He should be.

With the Word firmly engraved on the tablets of our hearts, are we not then prepared to be sent out to pour out Christ? ...invade earth by pouring out heaven? We're not gluttons feasting in the temple. We are fountains of living water... giving life to the dry and thirsty, giving the Bread of Life to the hungry. This is our passion. This is the fire that burns within us.

Is your "church" a fellowship for celebration, equipping and sending? Aren't we the church? Are we called to the Great Commission? Did Jesus preach in the temple? ... or did he go out and meet the people?

A tenth under law even in the time of Abraham, how much more under grace, mercy and love? It's all His anyway... including us.

Signs, Wonders and Miracles come when the Master comes... there's no formula... it's Him. It's always been Him. Yes, He sends us to do as He did, to work through us. And He adds greater things will we do. Got Jesus?

Milk is for the newborn, the young... meat is for the mature, those who have been prepared and equipped to be sent out. It's never been about numbers. It's always been about disciples... and disciples who make disciples... expanding the Kingdom... about souls.

The Bible makes a lousy armpit warmer... unless of course yours has an electric heater built in. It was meant to be opened... read... meditated upon... then shared with others who hunger and thirst for God.

Bread is for eating and the Bible for reading. Both are to be consumed. One feeds the body, one the spirit.

Romanticism (fantasy world of romance) with women is what pornography is to men. It is just as addicting. The concept of Holy Matrimony has taken a major hit. This is the strategy the enemy wages in the minds of people to steal the heart away from the concept of true intimacy, particularly intimate relationship with the Lord. These things are the enemy's counterfeit, to trap souls and steal them away from true Kingdom living. The counterfeits, romanticism and pornography, are addicting, because they never truly satisfy like real love. It's "never enough". This is war, the war on intimacy, the enemies' plan to stop a beautiful move of God toward the hearts of His children. But we are warriors. Victory is found in Christ.

The average age of first-time pornography viewers is nine years old. Celebrate Recovery group rooms for sexual addiction far outnumber drugs, alcohol and gambling... sex is today's drug of choice (self gratification). Interesting, considering the church is just now learning to walk in intimate relations with the Lord at this very hour. The enemy doesn't miss a beat. Our prayers matter... as Light gets brighter, the enemy is not sitting by idle. This is war.

Drugs, alcohol, sexual addiction and teen suicide are taking out our future generations before our eyes. What will it take to stir us to intercessory warfare to end this scourge? The church is not immune.

Suicide among pastors in America is at an all-time high. Sometimes we forget they are human just like us. Take a moment to pray for your pastor today. Go to him and thank him for his service to you and your family. Give him a word of encouragement.

Teen suicide attempts are at an epidemic proportion in America today. Bullying is said to be the main concern. Please seek the face of God for our future generations to turn back to God and undo what the government did by removing God from our schools. Jesus can win their hearts when they see His love in us.

Our lives as believers on earth should be a living testimony of the living God to the world as we release heaven on earth... and it's oh so beautiful... what an honour...

As true believers in God, we can be a living, breathing statement of the very life, breath, love and wonder of all that God is, to a lost and dying world. We have Him in us to do so, if we're willing to surrender who we are to be all that we can be in Him.

"Hold a church service and make converts"... count the sheep... Hold a fellowship service, equip and send the sheep to be the church, they make disciples who make disciples, and the sheep reproduce sheep who reproduce sheep 'til there are too many to count... become THE church instead of a church.

One who's foot has crossed the line may very well need to know the destination by which he approaches and the overwhelmingly hot climate there. Another may need to hear of the nurturing Love of God... we speak what we hear Daddy God speak... He knows...

Our presence as true believers should surely carry into a place the very Glory of God, and send the enemy scurrying for the exists. What we have should draw those who the Spirit wills...

Jesus said the Kingdom of Heaven is within us... Could revival be defined as a release of heaven on earth? Maybe God is actually waiting on us to "release what we have in us" for the next revival, while so many of us are waiting for Him to "show up".

If the religious only knew what they were missing... one direct encounter with God is all it takes... boom... wrecked for life... who will carry the presence of God to the world?

God can't be explained... experience can take you so far, but God is no one night stand, mistress or friend with benefits. How do you explain with words to someone about "knowing God for yourself, to walk, live and breathe in His glory... to soak in His Love... to be One with Him... to be saturated with His joy and peace"... wow... heaven on earth gets all over you... suddenly nothing else matters. You realize what you've been missing... your first love, in deep intimate relationship. It's an encounter with heaven. And some people might think you're crazy. They're right... we're CRAZY ABOUT GOD!

God, let my life pour out Jesus, like a wellspring of fresh living water... I want to be your waterfall... an oasis in the desert of life... for YOUR glory and praise.

Every day, I want my life to shout out who God is.

The anointing comes from a touch of God, alone. He knows us. We know Him. We are the lightning rod. He is the lightning... the power... the glory... the honour... forever...

The first Commandment of the Old Covenant is to firstly LOVE GOD! Commandment of New Covenant is: LOVE GOD. Understanding what it means to love God is knowing who we are in God and walking in intimate relationship with Him... Father and child relationship...

Loving God is a surrender of the heart where we give place to Him in all our being... where His will becomes our will... where our lives and everything we are, is found in Him.

In the toughest mountain pass, or the lowest valley... some might walk away... some might even give up on themselves... but there is the warrior, Christ, who will never forsake us. That's why we need His life source in us... to overcome the weakness of our carnal mind and nature.

If we truly understand who Christ really is in our lives, evangelism (being fruitful and multiplying) is inevitable. It's impossible to do anything but shout it out from the rooftops.

We pray for bread... but His desire is to provide a banquet table to celebrate us. Our capacity to love and be loved is a riverbed that needs to run deeper than our own natural understanding, and step into the supernatural. Because there is more... much more to be had of God. We have not seen all that God wants to pour in and through us. We've had only a glimpse actually.

Wilful sin in the life of a believer comes from loss of our identity in God, if even for a moment.

Trying to earn the free gift of salvation is like praying for God to do miracles with no faith to actually see them manifest. It's like eating fast food. We're full, but full of what? Our body continues to search for a nutritional source and still hungers. And so we get fat on dead works.

My disgrace for a share of His inheritance... this grace thing is amazing... but it doesn't end there... how can I not fall in love with the One who loved me first?

The CHRISTIAN JOURNEY can be defined in this: Lay down the carnal mind and agenda (crucified with Christ) and pick up Christ in all His fullness...

This world has nothing for us. But as believers, we have all the world will ever want and need... and we can't wait to give it away to all who will receive... it's fun... it's addicting... it's contagious... it's love...

Yes, I am honoured to spend my life wearing the Father's signet ring on my finger... His finest Robe around my shoulders... a Bride of Christ, made a King, yes, to share the throne of the King of Kings, who modelled how to lead as a King: as a servant, with towel and basin in hand... sinless and Spirit-filled ...capturing souls with the net of His Love, a fisherman of souls, pouring Himself out to all those who will receive Him... so Abba may enjoy them forever.

It is not to my glory, are you kidding? Who am I, but the Bride! See my Bridegroom, Christ the Warrior, who went to hell to take away the keys of sin and death that we might have life eternal, that we might taste heaven forever.. our Saviour, who, with His own Blood, voluntarily took our place on the cross, for a people so very undeserving... no, it is not my Glory... I am honoured to give HIM glory...

And yet, today, as I come to understand my intimate relationship with Jesus, the lover of my soul, I see with spiritual eyes that see the unseen... my desire, my fire, my passion. My heart screams for the joy of bearing fruit for the true lover of my soul, Jesus... I cry out, I labour, for souls, to be in abundance in my garden, tree limbs weighed down of healthy luscious fruit, branches bending, swaying in the winds of the Spirit of God... what will it take to get me there... to burn for sharing the Glory of God with others with full abandonment?

It is the burning desire of every heart to love and be loved. And what is love? See One, Christ Jesus, hands spread wide, and feet, nailed across a tree, publicly expressing His extravagant, outrageous passion and desire for His Bride... all His affection poured out for us... laying down His very life for us... yes, THIS is love... how can we do anything but be in love with this man?

Lord Jesus, You have taken me with vengeance, with violence, with jealousy in Your heart... for surely You will not share me with another... You have been longing for my love all for Yourself... You have captured all that I am... Your love is driven deep into my soul... Your banner flies over my heart... I belong to no other... it's You, it's only You...

My faith, my life is poured out in surrender, as a love song to You, Lord God... take all that I am, wash over me with Your red rain, Lord... Your presence, Your fragrance, Your heartbeat, are mine to keep... just as I am Yours forever and ever...

This is Daddy God's plan for you... this has been His dream all along.... That you are His. And He is yours... family... co-creators for the Kingdom... being the Bride of Christ, bearing fruit for our Bridegroom, for the Kingdom, a harvest of souls... what a glorious harvest it is...

What a blessing to be a spiritual waterfall, pouring out Jesus upon the face of the earth wherever we go... in the marketplace, at school, at work... leaving a deposit of the Spirit of God, of Heaven along our path. We are Kingdom Culture Life models, just as Jesus Himself was, multi-dimensional, in that the realm of Heaven is being revealed on earth in and through Christ in us, so that the world might also see Him who loved them first.

It is such a beautiful thing to understand the love of a Father for His children. Yes, the God of the universe loves you, His child... the Creator, the creation... receive it... walk in it... saturate yourself in it...marinade in it ... let His

Love pour over all of your being... Mmmm... yes, it's sticky gooey love, so if you touch someone else with it, well, you're libel to get it on them for life. It's fun, too.

You know, sometimes I so understand the concept of Jesus telling the disciples to cast their ship to the other side of the lake away from the crowds... or telling the disciples to wait in the garden and pray while He went to seek the face of God in the wilderness. Sometimes, He is all there is, He is all that makes sense at any given point.

Every area of my life that doesn't release the presence and very fragrance of heaven is ground needing to be conquered for heaven within me.

All I know to be is a fire-breathing Holy Ghost fire starter. Hey, it just kind of flows out of me, you know?

Catch a dream... make it real... placed in the hand of God, surely the impossible can be, if we will just believe. So I believe, like He believes in me... enough to surrender His only Son, as a ransom for me.

As I've come across many hurting believers during time of ministry, I've been seeing such a void of love for self in many. I see them taking up their crosses and pouring themselves out 'til there's nothing left, even to the point of them becoming rug mats to the self-seeking in their lives... family members, spouses, children, those in need of ministry, even pastors and churches who sheer sheep instead of feeding them. Sometimes a lack of self love will lead to enabling bad treatment by others. They might even feel they deserved the mistreatment... even joining in the mistreatment. And hey, guess what, I once fit right in with that, so I can so relate. I was taking on every and any ministry opportunity that crossed my path... and found myself completely poured out... not all bad, Jesus was still coming through full throttle... but it's a good way to leave earth prematurely. The point is I was trying to earn the free gift of God's love. But truth is, Jesus paid the price already. His work on the cross speaks of our value, our worth. We are no one's rug mat. Healthy boundaries are... well... healthy.

God's Love is not the same love as we know it... it is not of this world. As we pour out His Love, it GIVES energy and life, it doesn't drain us... "give and it shall be given unto you"... it doesn't say it will be drained from you.

Sometimes all we can do is pray... and then you pray some more... And after praying, you get on your knees and pray... and then on your face before your God... and you just know, in this time of fellowship with your gracious and merciful God, that the mountain WILL move... and the enemy will shake and tremble in awe at the power of Almighty God.

Christianity is about intimate relationship... the created to the Creator... family... it is not the seven steps to manipulating God into blessing us beyond our capacity to endure and persevere just because we want to be part of the "bless me" club... it's not the three step program to talk God into showing us favor, He already did that with Jesus on the cross... we're working THE Kingdom, touching the lives of others to bring them Daddy God encounter, not oppressing them with our kingdom within the Kingdom.

I will not be moved by time nor circumstance, but by every Word that proceeds out of the mouth of God.

Hey, no sarcasm intended here, ok? But if I hear one more "new grace" teacher, with *"THE ULTIMATE NEW AND IMPROVED MODEL OF GRACE, CALL THE NUMBER ON YOUR SCREEN AND ORDER NOW AND YOU'LL*

RECEIVE"... come on, man, seriously, we got to get over ourselves about what WE get, and get other's focused like Christ was... yes, grace is beautiful... but what commandment tops the old and new covenant? LOVE GOD. There is so much poured into that two word statement, wow...

When you are introduced to a pastor to join a team in a church and he tries to clone you into himself, then calls you rebellious for resisting and actually having a relationship with God yourself, hearing His voice with your own ears, and having an understanding of your spiritual gifts, don't be afraid to bless him with your absence on future Sundays. Some just don't get it. It's ok. Pray for them that they do.

When I look back at who and where I was in this life... and see where I am today... wow... I mean, if I wasn't hopeless, nobody, I mean ain't NOBODY hopeless. NOBODY.

God can be defined with a 4-letter word: LOVE

Make me a fountain of You... Lord, nothing else will do... All I want, all I need is found in You.

I know I have some wounds that need processing and maybe some situations to release to God when good things start to happen in my life and then some things start to surface that I didn't know were lurking down at the bottom of my riverbed. But when the cleansing work is done, there is Jesus... arms open wide, to remind me... I AM LOVED... and then there is room in my heart to receive to full capacity, all that God has for me... and there's always room for future expansion... because He is so good to me, and I am willing...

Sometimes when I slip into the mode of remembering tough stuff from my childhood, it's nice to have friends who remind me that I AM LOVED... and I can draw close to the heart of Daddy God and find peace, rest and healing there... for surely He is Father to the fatherless places in my life...

I'm not going to stop until Heaven is dripping off of me and religiosity is running from me.

Tears fall for the just and the unjust. Do we mourn for those who do us wrong? Are we quick to forgive? Does our love extend even to our enemies? Jesus loved Judas even to the kiss of death... I pray to God for revelation for a love such as this... that I can be a model of Jesus even to those who seek to do me wrong...

GRACE is NOT a license to sin... no... it's a license to be FORGIVEN... to be set FREE of the law of sin and death. SEE Jesus upon the cross publicly and passionately expressing His love for you, for me. SEE the empty tomb. SEE the keys of the law of sin and death in the hands of Christ that HE took from the enemy of God and man. Jesus DID NOT COME to abolish the law, but to fulfill it, as the flesh in us was too weak... but Christ, the precious, spotless Lamb of God, He paid the price... how could anyone turn away such a love as this. And what have we to do? Only receive of His free gift... wow... that is GRACE. How does our broken, undeserving heart respond to such a love as this?

Had a friend recently tell me he feels like a tree that's been hit by so many storms in his life, he thinks he has a lean. I told him I'm like a tree that's been hit by so many storms I was turned to dust, and now the winds have blown my dust particles all over and I can't find me any more... but I can find Jesus in my place... and that's a good thing... so I know I'm going be alright...

I trust You God to see me through... so I close my eyes... I step off the cliff of this life circumstance... into your hands I release my all... my very life... all my love... all that I am... take me... I am Yours... for You alone can make sense of me and bring to life Christ in me...

Sometimes I don't always understand... and I don't have to... I may ask, but I don't question. I may need to take some things into my prayer closet... but this I know... He is God... He is my God... and I surrender all things to Him... no matter what...

I don't always understand... but one thing I know, You are God... so I reach out to take Your hand, and prepare myself for the potter's wheel.... oh God, what have I to do but lay it all down before You... one more time... or however many times it takes, 'til Christ be formed in me...

The mind of Christ is concerned with the things of heaven. The carnal mind is forever earth bound. We do have a choice.

We must be found in the heart of God before we can be an ambassador of God's heart.

Once you truly know God and enter into deep, intimate relationship with Him, you realize it's a never-ending conversation that becomes your life.

Satan wants us dead so we can't produce fruit for the Kingdom of God. God wants us dead... dead to ourselves, so the Life of Christ can be made manifest in and through us and the Kingdom of God can harvest the bounty of fruit.

To know of God's unfailing, undying, passionate and intimate love for us can only saturate us with the joy of the Lord, building our strength. It is here we find ourselves as a tree, planted by streams of still water abiding in His Rest... yes, the River of God, full of free-flowing living water... and the love that transpires there bears fruit in its season. And our lives and ministry are fulfilled.

Our prayers make it to the throne room quickly when they're not weighed down by doubt and unbelief. Answers do come unhindered to those who trust God and understand their identity in Him.

Seeking God? Don't feel Him? The separation is on our part... because the Word says He NEVER leaves us nor forsakes us. He's always there for us, and willing to go as deep and intimate as we will allow. He won't force Himself on us ...He is a gentleman... but He WILL pursue us...

Deliverance accelerated: deep intimate worship that draws the very Glory of the Presence of Almighty God. It's amazing how fast darkness will flee. We just have to evict the trespasser, close the door, and keep the Light on.

Behaviour modification or personal choice cannot empower you to have the Life of Christ move in and through you anymore than a certain amount of bible knowledge... only surrender and direct encounter with God through intimate relationship can ignite such a supernatural transformation. He reveals His deeper mysteries to those whom he loves...

Walking with God with our arms open wide always looking to receive is a sign of immaturity. As we grow in intimacy and come to truly know God, we seek to be like Jesus... other's focused... understanding that as we seek the Kingdom, and we give, pour out, release heaven from within us... we trust God that what we need will also be poured into us. This is where our walk moves from being about grace, to a love affair with Jesus.

A more effective prayer life comes from seeing through the eyes of God. This supernatural occurrence happens through intimate relationship with Him... when we can tap into all that He is, through the Holy Spirit that He has sent for us.

The Life and Love of Christ can be released from within us when our love for God and Oneness with Him reaches such a level that it carries us beyond our natural selves, out of ourselves, and into the supernatural, stepping into all that He is and all that He ever intended for us.

Healing, deliverance, carrying and releasing the very presence of God... we can't but God can... I have to ask myself the most important question... is He or is He not living in me? If He is, we are empowered to step into all that Jesus did, and even greater things will be do...

The deeper I go in God, the deeper my riverbed is dug out and widened. Ouch. But is it ever worth it...

We were made for Love... anything to the contrary is toxic to our hearts...

Hell is a real place. Hell fire is a real consequence. Jesus paid the price and made the sacrifice. Be Jesus to someone today.

At some point we have to allow the fire of God to ignite who we were created to be in Christ. Souls are depending on us... and the souls those souls will touch... Each of us are important cells within the Body of Christ... we are family, we need each other...

When we discover who we are in Christ there is no going back... we've tasted heaven at that point... our destiny and purpose are in view and we just can't settle for anything less and be able to live with ourselves.

Sometimes I stare at the sky, glaring at the sun and wondering why. Then I remember Jesus is still on His throne... and I remember why. And that other thing that was bothering me... what was it again? I just don't remember. It seemed so important, but now it is so very forgotten.

People flock to prophecy because they seek a word from God... prayerfully the prophet's job is to help them establish or re-establish contact with God so they can hear Him for themselves... speaking here of establishing or re-establishing intimate relationship with the Lord.

Need a miracle? Be a miracle to someone else, and watch what God does in your own life.

Intimacy with God doesn't come from our efforts... it comes from our surrender... to Him, the One True Living God.

Grace is not only about what God will do for us, though the relationship with God has it's perks... but it is also about what God will do through us... a father teaches his son how to fish, eventually sending him out to fish for himself, and then someday He will teach his own son how, and they will teach their future generations.

Testimony assassins among Christians are an amazing breed and a growing sickness in the church. When reputation based on man (often-times gossip) outweighs anointing which is based on God, there is a problem. But who will stop a move of God and the destiny of one of His children?

What seminary or theology school do I need to attend to learn how to do what Daddy God does and say what Daddy God says?

We don't really need to explain God to people who don't know Him. We just have to introduce Him to them. The direct encounter they have will do far more than anything we impart of our spiritual intellect.

The more intimately deep in love we are with God, the more of Him we walk in to give and receive with others.

Love is a lifestyle. When it permeates every area of our life, it draws souls... like a net captures fish...

Some prophetic revelation is to be kept in the secret places of the heart and released only in prayer. Be slow to speak unless told otherwise by God.

Prayer is confirming God's will, in agreement with Him... and releasing the Power of God, with faith, to see it come to fruition.

Sometimes you just have to fly... others may not understand until they see the Glory deposit on your face when you return. Then they will understand where you've been and why. And they won't question you next time.

When I look back at who and where I was in this life... and see where I am today... wow... I mean, if I wasn't hopeless, nobody, I mean ain't NOBODY hopeless. NOBODY.

Ever feel like a rose?... trimmed from the bush for just such occasion... to fill someone's empty vase when they can't find someone else?... then left behind to be swept away with some old memory... love isn't about being tolerated... it is about being celebrated. If they truly love you they will care about your happiness.

Human Trafficking is real... it is happening right here in our schools too, with minors... some of these kids you wouldn't expect would fall victim to such a horror. We need to wake up, church, wake up, America... war is upon us... the enemy has his sights on our future generations... our children.

Half of the S.R.A. victims I've taken through deliverance were introduced to the Church of Satan by Associate Pastors of Christian churches. Their stories are horrific. Infiltration in the church is serious and it's real. We need to pray, church... we really, really, really... need to pray. This is war. And the enemy knows no bounds. I'm not calling for paranoid witch hunts, but for prayer.

2.8 million children and teenagers actually attempt suicide every year. The number one reason is bullying in school. Who's idea was it to kick God out of our schools? But of course, it all starts in the home. God move upon the parents, Lord... teach us how to disciple our kids.

There is a reason why the church of the Book of Acts operated in a successful economy... it was based on the concept of community and cooperation instead of under-cutting and greed as seen in capitalism... working together as cells within the Body of Christ might just work if we were willing... unity starts with love... Jesus commanded we love each other as He loves us, does He not? Love someone today... start a trend...

Have you ever noticed how few abortion supporters there are who have ever been aborted themselves and lived to tell about their experience and support of it?

I long for you, My Bride, to walk with me in the deeper places of all that I am... I have so much I want to show you... Will you come?

"Engage my heart in Yours... and Your heart in mine... this is the rhythm of Love... the rhythm of Oneness, with my Beloved... I can only cry... grieve deeply... as I am a lover separated from her Bridegroom... seeking in the dark of night for her one true love... and where can I go to be comforted? Nothing of this world can take away my pain... nothing else can fulfil the desire of my heart... neither power, nor wealth, nor wisdom... only Jesus.

Sometimes people, even pastors and a particular church membership, have to be pruned from our lives because they don't acknowledge our growth, are unable to provide what we need to continue to grow because it is not in them to give and we desperately need to continue onward in Christ. That's ok, it's just time to move on, maybe it's time for preparation of your own ministry, or God is calling you to a deeper walk. Some of these 'dairy farmers" can even be like a mother hen who only understands milk and feel you are being rebellious and desperately need their milk, or you will die without it... while we crave meat. Some just don't understand and think you belong to them and not to God. To stay is detrimental to the foundational health of the tree that is you. Love them where they are, but move to where God takes you. Dairy farms can serve a purpose for a season. Bless them.

Someone asked me where my church is that I pastor at... a few others stated they doubt I would make a good pastor because I'm so laid back and easy-going, the "artist" type. No, I'm not a jump up and down screamer type... some call that "fire preaching"... some of that is embarrassing to me actually, but hey that's just me... to think we have to manifest in the physical to create the power of God... I do like TD Jakes, he gets excited and lays it out there, boom! But he's not belting truth for the sake of belting truth, he get's EXCITED about it! Anyway, excited or not, it just takes God's touch, no matter what we do for the Kingdom or how we deliver it... from cleaning the bathrooms, to being a fountain of Christ and God's Glory from the pulpit. I've come into a room to share and the Spirit came before I said a Word. It's about God, not us.

There are testimony and anointing assassins out there, just waiting to be used by the enemy, to blockade your outflow of the River of God... well, they can try to disqualify you and the gift in you, but they can't disqualify the Gift-giver... your gifting will go forth and your destiny will be realized. Who will stop God? You didn't make it this far living by every Word that proceeds from the mouth of God, to be moved by words from the accuser that come from the forked tongues of men. Light causes every darkness to flee.

So often I have seen this... those that have jealousy issues who can't trust, turn out to be guilty of the very thing they are suspicious or even outright accuse their mate of. That is because they can't even trust themselves. Trust comes from love... if you can't trust yourself, how can you love yourself? If you cannot love yourself, how can you love anyone else? God is jealous for us, and won't share us with such things in our lives. His refiner's fire will bring the dross to the surface to be made known, so we have to deal with it.

What can we do when someone shatters our hearts with a hammer... and they keep doing it? We pick up the pieces and give them to Jesus so He can love us back together again. We forgive the offender, for they know not what they do, just as Jesus set the example on the cross and forgave us. We move on in the call of our lives in Christ. For we love and value ourselves and the anointing on our lives enough to say no to abuse. God paid a high price for us. We are precious to Him. Some may not see it, or choose to wear blinders. They labour against the Kingdom work within us because they are in bed with the enemy. But we are diamonds in God's eyes.

Bible knowledge and wisdom is great to have. It keeps the spirit fed, strong and in control of our lives. But fresh revelation comes directly from the mouth of God to those He knows, who incline their ears and eyes to Him. Do you know Him? Does He know you?

What seminary school, what theology college degree can teach me how to pour out Jesus to a lost and dying world? What school can teach me how to love with Jesus love? ...a love never before known by man... a love we can't even begin to comprehend... bringing heaven to earth... tell me... because THIS is what this lost and dying world desperately hungers and thirsts for.

In the quiet of my heart, I cry out my love for You... I can't stop the tears anymore than I can stop a mighty waterfall... tears of joy, tears of life... washing my heart of all that was, so I can receive all that is and is to come. All of heaven, fill my soul..

It's true, there's no room for religiosity in walking in the footsteps of Christ. The Spirit of the Living God is blowing away the chaff. The beauty of God is being released. Yes the enemy is resisting. But who can withstand the Lord? Have Your way, God... we invite You in. Consume us, Lord... all that we are is Yours.

Is it hard for us to figure God out... because He doesn't move the way we think He should? Let's not put Him in a box to try to conform Him to us... let's swing wide the heavenly gates and surrender ourselves to make ourselves just like Him.

How can I hunger for anything but to see the face of God?

Run the race, fight the good fight of faith... until you see heaven on earth being released. You will know at that point, your Commission is being realized. Then, the real work begins. As a carrier of heaven now, you will begin to see heaven invade the lives of those around you as well. It goes where you go. This is true Kingdom Culture living.

Stepping out of the boat isn't as scary as it may seem. Yes, He has taken you out into the deep. No, land is not visible from here. But He has you right where He wants you and only desires to see to the perfection of your faith. He wants all of you. Daddy God wants you to trust Him.

There are deeper places in God to be had for those who ask and earnestly seek Him. When He knocks at your door, will you answer? Will you step out of the boat and onto the water with Him?

When the wineskin of old passes away... and all is made new from within... count the old as loss in order to gain Christ. For surely the new wine of heaven is sweeter and God knows what you need.

My heart is aflame today. My oil burns brightly as I long for the embrace of my true love. My joy is found in ever-seeking the One who first loved me. He washes away everything in me that is not Him with His Blood, so that when I pour myself out, spend myself for the Kingdom... it is a pure offering of love I release to Him.

Do not eat from the table of religiosity, lest you become like them. It is the heart of God that tugs at you, that draws you away from them. For what form of truth or even honour and position, do they offer that can withstand the fire of God? On that last day it is you, the Bride, clinging to your Bridegroom, with all that is within you, being found in Him and He in you and you are One... that will stand before God. This is eternity' fulfilled.

The God of this vast universe adores me. His Son is in love with me... that, only my heart can comprehend. My mind cannot begin to understand, and asks, "Can it be? ...is it true?" ...as I look into the fire of His eyes of love.

God is my waterfall... a flow of endless love. I will never thirst again.

I am drowning in Your love, Lord. The air I breathe is no more. I breathe in only You. Yes, this life is over. It is Christ in me that is my only hope...

All I am, all I have is lost in You, Lord. There's no finding me now. I am consumed by You... it's You... it's only You.

Sometimes all I can do is melt in His arms and pour out all my love to Him. How can I be anything but wanting of my Lover, Jesus... in whom my soul finds my rest and peace!

What can I do when my soul cries out for heaven... when my heart cries out for my Lover? When I'm lovesick for my Bridegroom... and I awake, and yes, I am still here on earth. And yet, I hear His voice... and I know He is near. So i seek Him further still, in the quiet places, by the cool waters that soothe my soul.

Sometimes ministering to Christ is all I have room for... mmmmm. Loving Him there... wow. Once you've tasted true love, what else will you desire? Turn out the lights, light a candle, and well... It's Him and me... alone...

Stand... even when your heart stops, stand. No, it's not you. It's never been you. It's always been Him, in and through you. So what have you to fear? Even the tomb could not hold Him.

Sometimes we just have to cover our hearts, walk into the fiery furnace, and know that Love is waiting in there to minister life, even in the midst of it all. Hey, He is God.

It's the Glory of God shining in and through us, even from within us, that dispels the dark realm of this world from our surroundings. It sends the shadow running for cover, but has nowhere to hide. The Glory reaches even the farthest places of the earth. What shall stop the love and light and life of the Glory of the Lord?

I am Your waterfall, Lord... pour out Your river in and through me... make me all You created me to be... a garden of heaven to produce in abundance... take my riverbed deep, Lord... remove every rock, every stone that is me, because I want all of You... only You, Lord..

Lord, thank You for not giving up on me. You sent your servants to mentor me to be more like You... to peel away the layers of Todd to make me a diamond. I take up my cross Lord... shine all that you are from within me God. There's nothing I want more.

Could someone put on a groove beat, please? I want to get my Jesus Freak on...

My heart is still... for just one glance of You. The waters stir, all because of You. I can see the fire in Your eyes... burning with desire... The Groom longing for His Bride, whom He treasures... oh, for the love of His Bride... such love, so pure, so true.

Sweeter than honey on my lips... nothing more precious than my Saviour's kiss... so undeserved, and yet... never has there been a love like this... this fountain of joy overflows... the tears pour out all the more... tears of joy, when your eyes meet mine...

Captain of my heart... Keeper of my soul... In You I delight... It's You I adore... On the wings of the Spirit... I will take flight... lighting lamps... pouring out oil... cisterns are filled... water turned to wine... every heart on fire... singing the song of the Bride...

Faith is knowing as fallible man I am overrun... but in Christ I have overcome. To live is to die. To die is to live. So I surrender my life to take up the life of Christ.

One flame. Two hearts. Beating as one... not counting the cost. I lament here on earth for the life to come, that I'm longing for...

Is it me... is it You... if it's me, I'm breaking through... I have only one heart I'm breaking for. It's You... It's only You, God... I give myself as an offering... surrender my all 'til nothing of me remains. There's nothing of this life I could ever want more than You, God... it's You... it's only You...

Holy Spirit come and dance with me. Take my hand and romance me. I lay me down on the wings of Your love. Fire of God pour over me. Consume my all 'til only ashes remain. Lord, my desire is to be poured out for You...

beauty for ashes in the Light of Your Glory... I will surely be.

Upon this canvas is painted... the image of God: Bride and Bridegroom. The Master sets up His easel in the garden as the banquet table is prepared. This is the love story of our all ages... the love story of our hearts... that we might be found in Him.

True love is this... that in my fallen state, my flesh might pass away that I might have Christ... the free gift, living in and through me. Has there ever been such an expression of grace and mercy on earth? Man has never known such a love as this...

I will not settle for a little Christ here and a little Christ there... when it is convenient in my busy life. This is not balance. This is oil trying to mix in water. This is leaven in my bread... strange fire that only works to spoil the vine that is me. No, I want all, the Christ... until my last breath of earth becomes a breath of heaven and I am so lost in Him, I am no more... it is Him.

What must I do to walk in Christ... live, breathe, speak Him... that He alone pours out from my being. This is my passion, this is what I burn for. What else is there, for crying out loud?

Oh, man of the world I was. And yet the fire that consumes me, leaves no trace. For I have one desire... and that, Christ. For I have tasted heaven. Nothing else will do.

As I am pressed from all sides just as the olive is crushed for it's spoil, so it is that the life of Christ is made known unto me. For I am no longer of myself... I am One in Him in my passing... the Christ. Is this not the desire, the passion of every believer? ...the Bride, become One with her Bridegroom?

Holy Fire burn and consume in me all that is not You. Holy Spirit blow like a mighty rushing wind to remove the ash that remains... leaving only the beauty... and that, Christ... that it is not I that still has breath, but Him in me.

Was I not mad to think even for a moment that I could make it in this world without Christ? And now am I not mad with love for Him that I lose all, even life itself, to have Christ? What is this craziness I speak of? Are these not the words of a man so deeply in love he has completely lost himself? ...who is longing to be found in Christ? With a heart that burns, let me be found nowhere else.

Truth will surely find you out. It knows no bounds, including time. Eventually your heart is known before God and man, forever. And yet, the Blood... oh, the precious, cleansing Blood...

A strange brew may seem as relief to the sorrowful heart, but it's strange fire only prolongs their suffering and greets them in the morning like a thud. The issue that they tried to numb, remains. It stares plainly at them in the mirror.

Sometimes love isn't enough ...for some. But it doesn't mean you have to stop. They may walk away. So what? Love them right where they are, wherever they may be. If they purpose to offend, give them the other cheek too. But in the end, love will prevail.

Planting a seed does not guarantee a harvest. Planting no seed guarantees no harvest. You can do this... it doesn't take talent on your part for God to speak through you... just a surrendered heart and a willingness to fulfil your call.

Sometimes God denies us the very things we ask for... that will ruin His design that is us. This is love.

WHAT IS THE GREAT AWAKENING? It is the Kingdom within us that Jesus spoke of. For some, it is the lighting of our wicks, of our lamps... for some, the infilling with oil... others, blessing them with lamps as they come to know of God for the first time. Hey, it's TIME TO ROCK THE HOUSE! Anybody want to come out and play (come out of the 4 walls of the church and meet people where they are)?

When we walk in the light of the Lord to share the Gospel, a man's lack of approval, his rejection... is nothing to us. But the seed that we do plant in them takes. And when they hear the voice of God, the Word of truth come from our lips... and they are exposed to God's presence... perhaps we will get a chance to water.... perhaps even harvest. Maybe it is for someone else to harvest. It doesn't matter. What matters is that the soul is brought into the Kingdom... and we are unmoved... we cannot be shaken as fruit-bearers. We continue to work the harvest, regardless of the process and circumstance.

I have known what it is like to be wrecked in His glory... broken into pieces, ground into fine dust, particles blown all around until no evidence of me can be found. But hey, I'm still here... and I WILL see the face of God. What can I say? The tomb is empty. This is resurrection power. I am in Him. He is in me.

What is a ministry to the broken-hearted, except to find a heart surgeon to help put the pieces back together again? What is a ministry to the broken of spirit, but to mend the deepest places of one's being, to heal the breach, the effects of the betrayal? What is a ministry to the captive, lest you remove their enemy and set them free? What is a ministry to the sick lest we see them to their restoration? ...all of this provided by the work of the cross, if we can just walk in the revelation of it.

So your heart is wrecked. OK. God created it. He can heal it and put all the pieces back together again. It does no good to cover it over with a pretty carpet of fine works. The storm within will prevail. Open your heart and let Him in to those deep places in you. Speak to the storm "peace BE STILL"... and by the authority given to you in His name, the winds will obey. Just trust in that name.

Yes, it does hurt when we make ourselves vulnerable and we get wounded. But God didn't create us and fill us with passion and love to hide ourselves away in fear. The nails that held Jesus on the cross hurt Him as well. Wasn't it our sin, that held Him there? And yet, He pursues us even now... relentlessly. When our identity, self worth and value are found in Christ, the choices of others might sting for a moment... but they don't paralyze us. We forgive, place their sin on the cross just as Jesus placed ours on the cross, declare them forgiven as Christ did for us, and go on in the call of our lives to reach our destiny in Him. Tears are for the moment. Heaven is forever.

All that I am, all that I have is the Lord's. He is my Lover. What will I deny Him? Here I am God, have Your way.

Jesus, make us fountains of You... of Your Holy Spirit... Carriers of Heaven, releasing Heaven on earth wherever we go. Show us the glory of Your presence to manifest your likeness in us.

Many people contact me asking how they, too, can have an intimate relationship with God as they see in my life. If you, too, want this kind of relationship with God, then reach out to Him right now... take His hand and receive it... just receive the free gift of His love outpouring, His grace, His mercy. He loves us so very, very much... we can't even begin to have the capacity to comprehend it.

So often I have seen this... those that have jealousy issues who can't trust, turn out to be guilty of the very thing they are suspicious or even outright accuse their mate of. That's because they can't even trust themselves. Trust comes from love. If you can't trust yourself, how can you love yourself? If you can't love yourself, how can you love anyone else?

God's dream is that we might truly know and experience His love for us on a daily basis. He saturates us in it until it is dripping off of us and onto everyone and anyone who might cross our path. Hey, we can't help it... and oh is it fun...

Transition brings an end to one season and the beginning of another. In this case, death brings life. A seed falls into the ground and dies before it comes to life and breaks through the top soil to become all it was created to be. Ultimately, to bear it's fruit.

Sometimes it's best we don't always try to understand... because we may never understand... understand what was at work in the heavenlies at that time, both dark and light. You just love, and give the person or persons to Jesus and release and trust them with Him. Your glory train still has to move toward your destiny.

The love of God in us will wear out any enemy of God and man. But step into intimate relationship with God, and the enemy will run to the exits for cover so fast, it'll make your head spin.

From time to time I am amazed at what well-meaning Christians feel is the real deal concerning attaining the gifts of God. Usually it's that which was always presented to them and all they've ever known. And they will defend that stance no matter what. But, I ask, what theological seminary degree empowered Rodney Howard Brown to walk in such a rich Holy Spirit anointing that people drop like flies under the Power of God?... what college degree hanging on the ministry office wall empowered Benny Hinn's gift of healing? What theological school degree brought about the anointing that manifested a thick golden glory cloud over the worship service at Bethel Church in Northern California? When will we ever realize... it's not about what we do... though it never hurts to be proven studied and prepared... but the fact is, it takes a touch of the Master's hand. It's called an "anointing"... and God either gives it to you or He doesn't. It's no different than being an artist or a prophet. You either have the gift or you don't. You can refine it with study. But you can't "learn" to be an artist or a prophet. You either are or you're not. God can also impart a mantel to you if He so chooses... again, straight from the Master's hand. But to each He gives gifts. Find the one He has chosen for you.

If we're to be a citizen of heaven, we can no longer have the carnal mind at work in us, lest the world still have a grip on our hearts and manifest in our deeds.

All that God is fills in all that we are not. His strength is found in our weakness. When we are One with Him we are whole.

When my destiny stands revealed before me, what am I to do with my past? There's no room for it any more. I am filled with heaven from the top of my head to the souls of my feet. Sorry, no vacancies. Yes, it's true, Light is getting brighter. There is a renaissance toward the Book Of Acts church moving through the Body, and thank God for it. There are those walking in this new reformation. There are manifestations of God's glory moving through the body like never before... and yet darkness is getting darker. We're in a war, and our enemy would just as soon drag our souls to the pit of his eternal fire. But God has other plans for us.

As a fire starter, I carry matches for those whose light has gone out or never been lit... oil for those lacking the Spirit life and Kingdom reign anointing... even lamps for those who have yet to be introduced to the lover of their soul. The resistance is stronger than ever. But my passion is even stronger, and I see God building an army. They are His diamonds in the harvest fields, just as so many prophetically gifted saw months, and even years ago.

I am overwhelmed by Your Love, Lord... and what is my life to compare? Even if it were to end right now, I would simply fall into Your arms. And this, my life... yes, it is forever lost in You. And Your life, I have forever gained.

When reflecting on my prior substance abuse issues some 27 years ago before God invaded my life... and having worked with the severely disabled at one time, including some permanently damaged by substance abuse overdose... I realized that those disabled would do anything, pay any amount, to be able to live a normal life again. I also realize that substance abusers will pay anything to be like those who were disabled, for a temporary period of time at least. That seems to be the purpose of getting "high", even though they are taking a chance that the effect will be permanent... even risking death. I mean, seriously. Think about it. Is life really that bad that we need to be temporarily brain damaged to get through it? And that FEELS GOOD? We work all week long and look forward to spending the weekend brain-damaged? Really? And exactly WHO'S idea was this? Lord Jesus, please, empower our prayers, to end substance abuse in Your nations. Save us from ourselves, Lord. Bring an end to this scourge. Invade our lives that we ALL might know the joy and peace and love of walking with You.

Someone please call 9-1-1... Apparently I've been infected with a deeper, non-religious relationship with God. I don't think there is a cure. At least I hope not.

I have many bible translation books ... they are like different flavoured spreads for my daily Bread. But my favourite is the fresh revelation spread. You know, the one that comes direct from the mouth of God to enlighten my day.

I refuse to settle for a weak and powerless church. That's not what the Saviour gave His life for.

Anyone can read and know the Bible, even preach it... but to live it in its true meaning, is the life of Christ manifested in a beautifully surrendered soul.

When you're filled with the Holy Ghost... your lamp is lit and darkness now fears you. The heavenly dimension is now part of your life. The world may scoff at you, but you now have what they need. Offer it in love, with towel and basin in hand... just as it was offered to you.

I struggle with being a circle in a square world. I just don't fit sometimes. Then I realize... it's the world and religious systems that I don't fit into.. There is just no room for lovers of God. But hey, I DO fit in God's heart. That's what matters to me.

God doesn't ask us to understand His ways. But He does ask that we obey. It's about trusting Him totally and completely. It's a big step toward intimacy with Him. We got to know Him as Lover...

Why do we do what we do? It is our commission, it is our calling, we were chosen... to see the POWER OF GOD RESTORED TO THE LORD'S HOUSE. Wow, did you hear that? Was that thunder I just heard outside? Or was that the angels of heaven cheering that statement?

It is only natural for us as believer's to hunger for the supernatural. Our own transformation alone is a miracle in and of itself. We were absolutely swept away from the grasp of the enemy and into the arms of the lover of our soul. Now that we've tasted heaven, we want nothing else. It's kind of a sustained supernatural existence... where heaven and earth co-exist, collide...Two separate dimensions converge into one.

Nothing could take away all my pain. There was no way to overcome such a childhood. I was paralyzed by the grief. My body continued to age. My soul was stuck in time, trying to understand what had happened. Drugs could not numb it. Sex couldn't make it go away. Money didn't make it disappear. Materialism had no effect. Workaholism didn't touch it. Co-dependency was worthless. But God came and asked Jesus to carry it to the cross for me. Yeah... wow is right. What could I say... thanks? Are you kidding me? I wanted to know this man from Galilee... personally, intimately.

He captured my heart with His love at a time that I could only hate and revile Him. And yet He loved me right where I was. THIS is my God... who loved me first.

The mysteries of God are spoken in quiet conversation between God and His family.

Yes, it's hurts to dig our riverbed a little deeper. Ask a tree how it feels to be pruned. Ask Jesus how it felt to be crucified. Oh, but the fruit...

It's hottest at the tip of the arrow, where the fore-runner resides. The greatest pressure, the greatest warfare, occurs on the front lines of the battlefield. That's where diamonds are formed... so clear, you can see Jesus and His glory shining right through, unhindered.

Religiosity is unbelief masked by a truth... a counterfeit of faith mired in arrogance and pride. But it doesn't spell hopeless. Many religious in churches today will get saved. Someone just has to light their lamps.

The path to forever leads to two forevers. One for those walking in heaven on earth, and then there's the other. But it is forever nonetheless, with no end to their suffering.

We are born to live and serve our flesh and the prince of this world system, even the religious system if we so choose. We die to live and serve the King of all creation, letting Him live and reign in us, even in our time on earth in our earth suits. Whether we choose to live or die, when our time on earth expires, eternity will know us.

If you don't invite Him to the aftermath of victory... He may be hard to find when warfare strikes down the road. He's not a fireman. But He WILL relentlessly pursue you. So you know... give it up. He won't settle for anything less than all of you.

If you walk in ministry for the approval of men, you're in for a disappointment. If you walk in ministry in obedience to God, you will see the end of you that Christ might live and reign in you. The victory and glory is all His.

Feasting on the Word without a direct encounter with God is the dew of sweet honey that never touches your lips.

Hold on to the presence of God... let it permeate your being, run through your veins, invade your mind, will and emotions. Let it possess you. Hey, the worst thing that can happen is you'll be like God.

If we don't have faith for the impossible... have faith for God, who is more than capable of the impossible.

It's not ok to settle for being a pew squatter. What did Jesus say to the fig tree that gave Him no fruit?

With the Jesus Baptism of the Holy Ghost and Holy Fire (Luke 3:16) in our lives, we have what we need to take dominion in our lives and the earth. To taste the sweetness of heaven, be filled with the Word and God's presence, and serve it to others who hunger and thirst after Him. This is God's dream fulfilled... that we might find our way back to the garden with passion and desire in our hearts for Him.

I want my life as a Christian to be an open book of fresh revelation of the life of Christ.

Satan stands before us demanding we pay for our sins. Jesus stands before us saying, "paid in full". His Blood cries it out before Heaven and earth.

Religiosity is a counterfeit that sells the gospel of man to those who hunger and thirst for God.

When we come to the revelation that we are not all that... JESUS makes us all this. There is joy in taking up our cross and following in His footsteps.

The Love of God pouring out of us to the world is an amazing waterfall of life, joy and peace...

Do they see Jesus in us? ... in our attitude, our way of speaking to others? ...in how we conduct business? ...do they see His love? ...or did we leave Christ back at church on Sunday?

We are called, chosen, to be ministers of the Gospel... we ARE THE CHURCH. We are disciples commissioned to make disciples. We AREN'T called to hire surrogate fathers and mothers to do our works. It's not about pastor. He is there to "feed us" only, lead us to green pastures... and equip us as ministers ourselves to be sent out. And then we make more disciples who make disciples.

Church is inter-active and relational among the family of God It is not a building. It requires our direct participation... and not out of duty or law, but because we LOVE the One who loved us first.

Once we step out into the bearing fruit process... wow... our earthly lives are over. Welcome to heaven citizenship. Because there is nothing in all the earth like capturing a soul for the Kingdom. We got to give 'em Jesus.

Reading the Word and obeying it, prayer time with the Father, pouring into others, "the Great Commission", are added free benefits to help us experience heaven on earth. But they don't "earn" us heaven. You can't "earn" a free gift.

When you find yourself a passenger on the Glory Train of Life, you see God is the Engineer, and the way before you is Love... and God is touching lives through you and rocking your world... I mean, really, what could be better?...

Make me a fountain of You, Lord... nothing else will do. All I want, all I need is found in You.

How can I but long for the One who stole my heart on that miraculous day all those years ago, knocking the world right out of me? How is one supposed to ever recover and be normal again? All I can do is long for my Lover. And so I wait... with excited anticipation, I wait.

I can feel a breath of heaven under my wings. I can feel healing as You breathe new life into me. This is no dream, it is real. So undeserving, yet You were poured out for me. And so I run... I run into Your arms. Yes, into the arms of love I will run.

Sometimes I just can't quite function in this life... and I have to run into God's arms. I have no explanation for this. But i think it's normal. It's called rest. It's called love.

What is Christianity really all about? Love. Can it possibly get any simpler or more beautiful than that? Jesus said "love God and love each other as I have loved you." Love is an action. Have we shared the love of Jesus today with someone?

If you look for me today, you won't find me. I'm nestled, hidden in Daddy God's heart... mmmmm...

I must be doing O.K. The Word says judge a tree by it's fruit. I look in the tree that is me, the garden that I am, and I see fruit. But make no mistake, I know it is to God's glory.

Sometimes i just need to let out a cry... sometimes i need to just sing. Sometimes i need to scream it from the rooftops. However I say it, the message is the same... my heart is for You, God... I love You... this place in my heart is for only You...

Are you hungry?... Are you thirsty for intimacy with God? Well come and see that the Lord is good. Eat and drink and be filled... and know the joy of pouring out to others what has been poured into you. As you touch them, you touch the Heart of God.

It would be nice if this was easy... but this Christianity walk is a war. Everything inside of me is screaming a war cry: "HOLY!! GOD YOU ARE HOLY!!"

Anything I claim to be outside of the Bride of Christ united as One with Jesus, is something I need to crucify. Yes, there is ministry, art, music, photography... a result of a big Heaven deposit entrusted to me. They are His talents that I am to invest for His interest, His glory. But this is my target, this is my aim: Christ in us, the hope of glory. What else is there in eternity? What else is forever?

It's easier to work all day and pay the ministry staff to work the Gospel for us... then to be a minister of the Gospel and answer the call of our own commission. But now that I've crossed over and seen the miraculous power of God's Love... now that I've seen hearts changed, lives saved, people healed and delivered... I mean, I've tasted heaven. How can i ever go back? And if He can do this through me, imagine what He can do through you. This is how we minister to Him... pouring out the same Love to the world that He first poured into to us to bring us to life... loving others as He loves us.

When we open our mouths and Jesus speaks... when we reach out our hands with the healing touch of Christ Himself in us... this is what we live for now. It is the new life in Christ, with purpose. This is being One with the One True Living God.

I can feel heaven. I can feel You in me. This is no dream. This is You... and yet it is me... as it was always meant to be, Lord... Oneness... Bride and Bridegroom.

I am completely lost in the fire in Your eyes. They can look, but they won't find me, until they find You.

I'm not going to stop until heaven is dripping off of me, and religion is running from me. Then I'm going to pour it all over you. And you can go pour it all over someone else... and start a heaven epidemic.

Love doesn't hurt? Tell that to Jesus hanging on the cross.

We are circles in a square world. Our reasoning and wisdom doesn't fit the lifestyle of the world. Their lifestyle doesn't fit our theology. But love is a universal language everyone speaks and understands and is the inroad to every heart.

Please don't tell me about my sin. I already know. Tell me about Jesus and His undying, unfailing love. And so the world cries out. Can you hear them, can you hear the silent voices, too? They are longing to return to the garden with Daddy God, whether they know it or not.

The definition of the prosperous, abundant life: I have Jesus. Everything and anything else, is perks of that relationship.

Sorry, there are no formulas. To walk in intimacy with God, we just have to surrender to Him. The rest falls in place naturally through the flow of His Love to His children, and we fall in love with Him who loved us first. Will we let Him in? ...I mean, really let Him in, to every part of our being? ...Yes, I mean like possessed by Him... I don't know about you, but I want all of Him. I desire, I burn, I yearn for nothing less.

Cope and numb?... or overcome? ...psychology or relationship with our Creator? To truly overcome what the world might throw at us, we need the One who overcame the grave... the One who went to hell so we could have heaven...

Bride and Bridegroom are joined as One. The Bride, made spotless by the Blood of the Lamb... so that once again we are the image of God in intimate fellowship with Daddy God... in fullness. It is our destination fulfilled... the living water that pours out of us turned to wine. Let the wedding celebration begin.

Being crucified with Christ is not fun. But the journey in resurrection power is worth it all.

Truth: I try not to sin to save myself from eternal fire. Deeper Truth: I love Jesus so much, I choose not to sin because I don't want to hurt or defile my Lover, my Jesus. But if I do miss it, I run to Him... oh, how I run to Him...

What do you do with a Judas in your midst? Well, the truth is, it is Christ they attack. And who can stand in the face of God? Judas finally hung himself. But Jesus still loved him to the end (Matthew 5:44), even to the kiss of betrayal, the kiss of death. Jesus saw His Father's purpose in the betrayal, in the betrayer. What the enemy meant for evil, God used to save us all. The Lord knows... He knows.

Pouring out "our acquired wisdom and knowledge" filtered from the Word through us is great. But people need Jesus, not us. We become a conduit, a lightning rod for heaven to be poured out on earth... and the thirsty are filled to overflow and then they also pour out to others. This is the message for today... this is the walk of the Kingdom Culture. It really ISN'T about us. That's not just a saying, it's the message of the hour as our Saviour draws near.

The time of the release and discovery of the deeper things of the heart of God is upon us... as we grow closer to God and He draws near. Over time, like fine wine, the flame of romance ever increases. It is made to burn forever.

How did I know your need? Well, God knows... I'm His lover. We have no secrets. I can't possibly understand all that is God. But I can believe and trust and love... love Him with all I have. He is Daddy... He is my God. He is my all in all. He lavishes me in love and life and happiness. My gaze is set upon Him. I melt in His arms. His heartbeat rocks my world.

Faith serves to take areas of my soul to the foot of the cross and leave them there. A valuable diamond is not clouded with self.

Homesick for heaven? Lovesick for Jesus? Join the crowd, there will be more and more of us by the day... face-first on the ground, crying out for His long-awaited return.

A fully-surrendered soul cannot resist a direct encounter with the Lord. You may feel like a mess for awhile, but when the dust settles, wow. Prepare for the time of your life. You will never be the same, never look back. You won't want to.

Renewed people create renewed people, create a new heritage, a new legacy. They soar far above the limits of this world. Eagles weren't created to dwell inside four walls.

The Holy Spirit of God wants to be released from within you. So let go and release heaven... and watch it overtake your family, your city, your state, your nation for God. PARTY TIME!

Fear looks like a safe place to hide... until you realize you misplaced your faith. It takes love to find faith... love for the One who loved us first. Perfect love casts out fear.

Our destiny is God in us, released, empowered and uninhibited... and all that comes with it.

Breath of heaven, pour out on us right now. Holy Fire of God light us aflame for You. Holy Spirit ignite us. We want to play, Daddy... oh, how we want to come out and play.

Sometimes a heaven work will appear to be impossible... and sure enough it will have God's fingerprints all over it when it is accomplished... and the world will look at us scratching their heads. Isn't this fun?

It's just a mountain, it's ok... it will surely move. It's not about what you do to make it move at all. It's "Papa God Time". Assume battle position - on your knees, on your face... carpet time... and pour out your heart. He didn't pay such a high ransom for you to forsake you now.

As a minister of the Most High God, if seeing a soul touched by the Lord in and through you doesn't move you... well... then ask God for a match, a new wick, oil refill, a new lamp... whatever it takes... but ask... fervently... even desperately... and check for a pulse if you have to. But do it.

Heaven is forever. Forever is heaven... flowing from you to me, me to you, us to everyone we encounter. Is there anything more beautiful?

The past DID happen. Denial is NOT an option. The Blood of Jesus IS. Love is healing. Healing is amazing. He provided His very life source... we just have to saturate ourselves in it.

Religiosity has not known a direct encounter with God. It dies in the Light of the Glory of His presence.

The riverbed that holds the Love of God is so much deeper than we could ever understand or imagine. How could we ever paint this image, or sing of such beauty? ...it begins in the womb of our rebirth and runs to eternity touching so many hearts along the way... if we'll just allow His heart to beat in us. This is the life source, THIS is what we were created for, THIS is our destiny, the Great Commission. THIS is HIS glory, found in us.

The hope of all hope is found in knowing God, intimately.

There are dimensions and places in God He longs for us to explore. He is drawing you out into the deep, to the perfection of your faith.

Daddy wants us to financially prosper. This is fine, until it becomes us. Then it's a problem...

What does your heart beat for? Spend yourself on that which is forever... because tomorrow just may be the first day of eternity, and souls are at stake.

The things of the earth will be long forgotten. Pour out Jesus into someone's life and watch the effects transform them for eternity. They aren't the only one's who will be touched. Watch what it does in your own life as well.

Your prayers will release to others that which is in you. We cannot afford to be filled with anything but Jesus.

Most scripture concerning financial prosperity contains the word "obedience"... that should speak volumes to our hearts...

Passion is born of fire... holy fire or strange fire. What we burn for depends on our focus... self or others. The Love of God is all about blessing others. The world is about the "bless me club". Want to walk in prosperity? Bless someone today.

The deeper mysteries of God are made known to those who are known... by God... His family.

Jesus is within me, yet i am found in Him. The Spirit also dwells in me. I am His temple. My heart song is heard in the very heartbeat of heaven... where heaven and earth converge... this is heaven on earth.

The Kingdom of heaven waits to be awakened within us. So we strike a match, ignite the wick, and enter in... with fire and passion for God.

I will not be moved by time nor circumstance, but by every Word that proceeds from the mouth of God. Not my will, Lord, but Yours be done.

I trust that somehow, some way, the God of the whole universe, is big enough to watch over all my affairs. Of course He is. I can be so silly sometimes.

Some of our greatest victories come while we are in a state of rest... because it is in that place that our trust and faith are energized. We KNOW God is big enough to cover us, so we lay down our lives completely in Him... let the enemy rage against us in the watch of Daddy and watch what happens. The enemy will wish he never messed with us... wish he never knew our names.

What else can I do but adore Him? What else is there? What else do you say of the One who is your all in all? His very love is sweeter than life itself.

Beautiful? You are more than beautiful in His eyes. You're so precious He surrendered His only Son to pay a ransom for you. His love is a deep riverbed that flows with His grace and mercy for a people so undeserving and yet so loved.

Yes, the grave still sits empty today. No, He isn't there... only a deposit of His unfailing, undying love can be found there...

Indeed we are a peculiar people... understand this... we don't fit in this world... and that's actually a beautiful thing. As citizens of heaven on earth, we're not supposed to fit here. We're supposed to bring a release of heaven to the earthlings so they become like Jesus... not try to fit our circle in their square. We just need to maintain our circle and move closer to Jesus everyday so we're pouring HIM out, not pouring us out.

We only deserve because of Jesus. He deserves anything good, and He lives in and through us. THIS is the prosperity message... not a measure by our bank account or possessions, but by the death and resurrection of Christ in us.

Love is a choice... DEFINED: love Jesus so much that sin is not even a choice…. where reverential fear of God is been engraved on our hearts.

It's not about the reward we get for serving Jesus. Jesus is the reward. Of course, He will adorn His bride. But, that's the difference between truth and deeper truth... we are in love with Jesus... we are His Bride. Religion is in love with the reward and their own honour, the "bless me club"... building their "kingdom within the Kingdom. They don't understand intimate relationship with Daddy God, taking grace to the next level, into His love… it's a deeper understanding that needs to take place.

You can always tell a religious spirit. Their hidden agendas give them away.

The glory is the Lord's. He will pour out what He desires to pour out. My eyes are fixed on Him, not what He gives, though His grace is beautiful indeed… but Him. I want Him.

There's nothing fun about having to love the unlovely… especially when the unlovely is me. I once heard my last mentor describe "vanity" and being "self-absorbed" as being "infatuated with one's own belly-button". I haven't laughed that hard in, well, ever…

My soul burns for You. My passion is for only You. My gaze is upon You and only You. How can I ever go back? Life will never be the same… thank you, God.

Sitting or leaning on our laurels only serves to stunt our growth and steal our next experience with God. Truth is there's more to be had of God… there's always more. He is never ending, far-reaching, always expanding… from the beginning and extending the ends of the earth. He loves to share His garden with His own.

You know you are home when you are celebrated, not just tolerated. This is the desire of Daddy God.. to celebrate us, celebrate every breath we take, our every heartbeat…

As I've walked these latter days of my journey, I'm beginning to understand the importance of Philippians 3:10-11… to understand we have to die in order to live… the death of the carnal mind, crucified with Christ, and taking up the mind of Christ. This is life. This is where it all begins…

When we look inside ourselves in times of deep reflection… when we look at our brother… our sister… when we look at the news… what do we see? Yes it can be hard… And what of the human condition? Did Jesus not come as mortal man to set the example? And we, as the Bridegroom that we might be His Bride, thus completing the image of God? Yes, it requires that we walk upstream, against the tide… live as circles in a square world, a peculiar people, exposed to persecution and even friendly fire from the religious… but to live in the Glory of God, wow. If you've tasted heaven… you know there is nothing in this world that can compare… and so we surrender, we lay down our lives, to let the life of Christ rule and reign in us. We take dominion as sons, and rule as servants... bold as a lion, gentle as a dove, overflowing with the Love of God that flows freely to those who hunger and thirst after Him.

GRACE OF THE CROSS: Daddy provides child a brand new bicycle. Child rides and enjoys bicycle. Yeah, child hasn't been doing chores and schoolwork as promised. BUT DADDY LOVES CHILD SO MUCH HE SENT HIS ONLY SON TO TAKE THE DISCIPLINE FOR THE CHILD.

2.8 million youth and teens attempt suicide every year in this country. That is ACTUAL ATTEMPTS. The biggest reason? ...bullying. Could some atheist please explain to me again why we had to remove God from public schools?

Some people are astonished that I speak of "pouring out Jesus" to others as being what CHRISTians do... well, I don't see MY name or YOUR name in the word CHRISTIAN, do you? What else are we going to do? Sit in a pew with our best smelly on and wear a groove in a pew in the same spot in a church building for the rest of our lives and look pretty, thinking' that's going to get us to heaven? You're kidding, right? I want some CHURCH my brothers and sisters... let's go kick some devil butt...

We don't need to concern ourselves with building a kingdom within the Kingdom, to serve as a platform for ministry. If we just focus on pouring out Jesus, the Kingdom will build itself around Him.

I can't relate to people with an agenda for doing ministry. I have a Lover. His name is Jesus. I want to bear His children. It's only natural. It is instinct, like any wife who wants to bless her husband. There's no agenda... it's just Kingdom Culture Life... the Great Commission fulfilled. So we go soul-fishing. We present souls to our Bridegroom. The Kingdom is expanded. This is it. This is where it's at.

When "church as usual" makes you... well... (I could use stronger words but I won't lest I offend)...
"uncomfortable"... when a house seems to go from the latest and greatest to the next fad teaching (latest best-selling book, popular speaker) and nothing really sticks... maybe it's time you go BE the church... with love... and just pour out Jesus o...n some people. He is the author

and finisher of our faith. Trust me, they will get Him. It's hard not to when He's living inside of you and you feel His heart beating in yours.

TRUTH says we have to do more repentance, more time in the scriptures, more time praying... tasks that are great stuff that build up our Spirit to walk in God. We pour out our knowledge of the principles of the Lord as well as we can in our human state. DEEPER TRUTH says we pursue God and He pursues us... we spend more time in scripture and prayer because we want to be with our First Love... and HIS HAND is upon our lives, invading our world, making the impossible not only possible, but the norm... because JESUS lives and reigns in and through us. We pour out Jesus, not our knowledge of Jesus. It's not a task, it's what we burn for... it's our passion. THIS is Kingdom Culture Life.

When we surrender, we become at peace with God... anxiety and fear find no place in us as we realize, He loves us right where we are... and our spiritual atmosphere clears.

Honour is found kneeling at the feet of those you disciple, with basin and towel in hand.

There's no looking back at the former trials lest we let yesterday steal our today and tomorrow.

A special THANK YOU to the armed forces of the United States of America... past and present... who have stood and fought for our freedom and liberty. God bless you and be with you all!!

How can our mind fully comprehend a work of the heart? We step out in faith in obedience to God because we trust in Him alone. Stepping out of the boat and onto the water, requires stepping out of the natural mindset and into the supernatural. This requires a trusting intimate relationship with Daddy God.

God's Love for us is EXTRAVAGANT! It's OUTRAGEOUS! It's, it's, well... it's Jesus... on the cross... stepping out of the tomb... coming out of the gates of hell with the keys of the law of sin and death in His hand... His eyes of fire, fixed on us, His Bride. Us, Him, in the garden. He wraps His arms around us... true love's eternal embrace. Come Lord Jesus, come... tarry no more.

God places His hand on our works and then rewards our fruit. God also chastises those whom He loves, then pays the penalty Himself so we can continue our journey. Can you say favour? Isn't grace amazing?

Fear is the opposite of faith. It will steal your inheritance if you're not careful. Faith is found in Love. We trust the One we love, the One who loved us first, and have the faith to know He will fulfil His promises.

Honour and anointing comes to leadership with the biggest basin and towel.

How can I feel, when my heart is shredded and torn... How can I find my way in this world, except You light my way... you wrote it in Blood, wrote it in Blood, how much You love me, how much You love me... you wrote it in Blood, wrote it in Blood, how much I really mean to You. I am simply lost in Your love, this I cannot deny. I am a circle in this square world. I don't fit, and I won't even try. So, I'm holding on... to what I know is real life. Yes, I'm holding on... to You. It's all I know to be real... all I know that will be here... when forever comes.

The Son of the God of the Universe is coming back to earth for His Bride, the church... to marry us, to marry YOU... yes, that means you're engaged, that you have a fiancé... and yes, that is His ring of love on your finger... that is His song that He sings over you...

It really takes reprogramming to step out of the world system, the carnal mind... and make Jesus Master of your heart, mind, soul and spirit... and let His Love do what it does. He will take your hand, and romance you into your eternal destination, one heartbeat, one breath at a time.

Believe and it shall be. You've taken the first step... the battle of the mind. Invite the Lord into your thought life and watch heaven come down and overtake your world, so that it operates as it was created to be.

Spiritual gifts without fruit are like having a shed full of Daddy's power tools. But they never get plugged in...

He loves you with passion... with violence. He will pursue you. He is a jealous God and will not share you with any other.

Tree branches don't enjoy being pruned, ...nor do they see the reasoning behind it... until the harvest.

Make no mistake... we are a treasure to Christ. He gave His life voluntarily that we might once again know the passionate love of the Father.

Ignition is coming... lamps, oil, matches... BRING IT ON GOD!!

My prayer is that people have to find God to find me... that I have nothing to pour out but Jesus.

And so I bare my soul in total surrender... what else is there to do? No, I'm not going to step over the bow and carefully walk onto the water... I'm going to jump in!... and run into His arms of love... because that's my Jesus. If I don't have Him, what do I have?

True love doesn't acknowledge walls. It passes right through them. True love doesn't know death... it denies it power and gives life. It is the heartbeat of everlasting life. It never stops.

Man's Gospel of me, myself and I is being exposed before God and man, by the Holy Spirit. God is simply ironing a wrinkle in our theology. Christianity is not about a focus on self, what we get. Grace is awesome, and we are grateful to God for it. But Christianity is being others focused, not just receiving through grace, but giving it out to others as well... living it ...loving it... loving others as Christ loves us. We all have to make a choice as to where we stand. Prospering by the Hand of God is awesome. The form of intimacy, giving or doing to get, is the principle of prostitution. Intimacy, giving or doing from a heart of love is having the nature of God. It's all about the heart.

To know the Father Heart of God... mmmm hmmm... I'm living, dancing to every beat... it is my life's pursuit.

The most awesome thing I've found in this intimate relationship with God... is He is inside me, at all times. Yes, He will be quiet at times... when He's letting me work through things myself. But the Word is true. He never leaves me nor forsakes me. I call this life of never-ending fellowship a "life of prayer"...I wouldn't want it any other way. I can never go back. I want Him by my side, always in ongoing fellowship, ongoing intimacy.

I don't know about you, but I am holding on to the hem of His tallit and refusing to let go until He heals the very life source itself within me... until I am no more and He is. THAT is healed... THAT is being whole.

We are citizens of heaven, aliens to this world... we've stepped into the super natural even though we're still living in the natural. Heaven overshadows earth in and through us. Focus on, cultivate, water and feed only that which you can take with you to your final destination. The rest will fade away regardless.

Yes, Jesus died 2000 years ago to pay the price for our sins. Acknowledging that when we discover we missed it on something is only part of faith application. Faith without works is dead (James 2:17). There still may be a need for inner healing, and even deliverance. These applications, the Bible calls elementary (works of repentance, Hebrews 6:1-2). Is there still a need for repentance once we accept and receive the work of Christ on the cross? Well, do we still sin? Or is it magically an automatic work of the Blood? No, it's still a relationship with Him... so run to Him, run to your lover, run to your redeemer. He will meet you right where you are.

There is a reason why Jesus expressed to us the need to pray when we pray, "forgive us our trespasses" and "deliver us from evil", in the Lord's prayer. Grace did not give an automated ongoing repentance that comes with automated forgiveness.

There are many realms of a person: body, mind (soul) and spirit. No, the demonic realm cannot dwell where the Holy Spirit dwells, but they do latch on in other areas of our being... flesh, etc. Is it oppression? Is it possession? Call it what you will or however it fits your theology (which to be honest matters not)... just kick its butt right on out of there.

No, we do NOT frustrate grace and try to force people under law again, where the enemy can accuse. There is a place for relationship with the Father Heart of God, to repent, be delivered, apply the work of the cross and the empty tomb... and reconnect with Him, and remove the leaven, the sin tendency, even spiritual open doors. Law is no more, it is fulfilled in Christ, the lover of our soul. That relationship alone replaces the carnal life.

Just as Jesus said "I did not come to abolish the law, but to fulfil it" (Matthew 5:17). Walking into the deeper things of God (Hebrews 6:1-2) builds on a foundation (the resurrection of the dead, laying on of hands for healing, and cleansing or consecration)... of the temple of the Holy Spirit that is us... the garden that is us, the tree (ministry) planted by rivers of living water that is us ...and empowers and enables a harvest of abundance of fruit in our branches.

Surrender is this place of acceptance and understanding that it's about the touch of the Master's hand, not about what we can do, but what He did, on the cross. He then enters into the situation, just as He lives inside of us.

God will have His way with you one way or another... might as well wave that white flag sooner than later. It's ok, He just wants to whisper in your ear how much He loves you...

Do this, don't do that, or you're going to hell!! ...is a lot easier to preach, than the love, grace and mercy of God. Preaching and teaching the loving kindness of God takes faith.

Well, He took the extra time for me, so my time is His. He gave His life for me, so My life is His. Take me Lord... I want nothing less than to be Yours for eternity. If You can transform ME, Todd L Thomas, no doubt, NO ONE is hopeless, Lord.

Yes, I have seen that tunnel... with the light at the end... multiple times. Two heart surgeries, cancer... just wasn't my time. TOO MUCH FUN TO HAVE WITH DADDY GOD HERE ON EARTH!! That's why I live as I do. What have I to fear, what have I to lose? I lose my natural life, I gain eternal life... real life... Woo Hoo!! Summersaults and cartwheels. JESUS, I LOVE YOU SO MUCH!! Wreck some people's lives out there today for Your Kingdom... Turn their lives upside-down so they are right-side-up again, Lord... Drown us in Your oil of joy, in Your Love, in Your presence, God. We can't wait to melt in Your arms, Lord. Steal our hearts away, God. Our affection is for You, only You, Lord.

He died for our sins, for our healing, to set us free, 2000 years ago. He alone can fill the void in our hearts we were born with... to restore us to Daddy, Papa God. Take us back to the garden with Him. Jesus made a way where there was no way.. Believe me, I've searched the world over, tried it all... everything the world has to offer. Jesus is all there is that satisfies, that will ever fill that void we are born with from our exit from the garden. Hey, don't take my word for it, go to Him and see for yourself... see that indeed the Lord is good. His loving kindness is beautiful and His Love never fails.

How can I ever look upon Love... the Man from Galilee, nailed to the cross, a mass of shredded Flesh and Blood, the precious Blood... and not know His Love for me? He took my place there on the tree. Yes, I died that day some 2000 years before I was born, because He paid it all. And now I am alive, born again in Him, and He is in me. I will settle for nothing less.

Sometimes as ministers, we slip into the harvest field labors in our own strength, wisdom and knowledge... sometimes without knowing it. We even try to earn God's love through works and service (how do you earn a free gift?). If we'd just surrender and let God love on us and the person we're ministering to, and let Him do what He does. The wineskin isn't to be tasted. It is the wine that is good.

Just because they show you the door doesn't mean seeds weren't planted. Just keep moving, keep planting, keep watering, keep pouring out Jesus...

I won't stop dancing... even if I cease to exist'... I won't stop dancing because I just can't resist... because I've got something to jump and shout about. I've got something I want to scream about. There's a love... there's a love, who knows your name. Yes, I said there's a love... there's a love who knows your name... and His hand is reaching out, will you take it? His heart is reaching out, yes that's your heart, breaking for His... and there's no way... there's no way... to stop the dancing, the dancing... there's no way, there's no way, to stop the dancing, the dancing... because He's captured you... you're not yours anymore... He's captured you... and He's yours from now on...

You know when the evening's gone... and the city is done with her song... the night light of the sky is all that shines on my face... but I'm never alone, never in fear... except to tear your sweet caress from me, would be all i could take... stay with me my Love... walk with me, in the moonlight tonight... like a candle in the wind, i will bring You, to where only angels dare to go... soul to soul, heart to heart... you burn bright, completely poured out... in the secret places of life... Your Glory is known even in the deep... even in the deep... and I watch... as the darkness cannot run away fast enough...

If you, turn and walk away. If you tear yourself in two again. Well, don't look now, because you won't know how it could be, but you're really not alone. You're heart still beats and He's come to put you back together again. Yes it's true, it's really you. Yes, it's you and Him alone again... singing in this night... of tears and pain, the falling rain, and it really doesn't matter. What's done is done... and life travels on. You've a race to run before you. No you're not done. A great destiny stands before you. He's got you in His arms... and He's never letting go... never letting go. He will kiss your tears that fall like rain... fall like rain. He will kiss the tears that fall like rain... fall like rain. He will kiss the tears...

We just have to be Jesus to people, He will do the rest... at whatever time and whatever place and through whatever spiritual gifts He desires. We just have to be available... be the diamond jewel so He can shine His glory in and through us uninhibited.

We receive and operate in our gifts by giving people Jesus... our Spiritual gifts, along with signs, wonders and miracles following. Yes, we who believe were bestowed with, ALL these gifts because Christ is alive in us and He walks in all of them. He operates in certain gifts through us more than others by His choice, our given spiritual DNA.

It's NOT what we do, but what He does. This does not mean the other gifts in us are null and void. Our arsenal is lacking nothing, in Christ, as mentored and imparted to us by the Holy Spirit.

So they hand you the microphone and you deliver the Word of the Lord and the presence of the Spirit of God fills the house... people are touched... and they ask you not to return. Obviously there are houses of man and houses of God. Some pastor's (and their wives) can't handle someone else being the voice of the Lord in THAT house, because somehow they mistakenly feel it is THEIR house. And if someone is going to speak, it HAS to be them. That should be a clue to you whether God is really welcome there or not. Don't be offended. It's not about us anyway, right? Dust off your feet and go to the next house. God will deal with them in due time. The husband is to wash His wife in the Word. The Bride, the church, is the wife of Christ. He is the husband, not us.

Time taken for those fruitless branches with hidden agendas steals from the branches that bear fruit... and then both suffer. We owe it to the tree (ministry), and the Master Gardner, to prune.

Hebrews 6: 1-2 warns against falling repeatedly into the cycle of repentance. On Sunday do we prepare to "go to church", and then back into the world for the week until next Sunday's spiritual Blood bath of repentance. What's wrong with this picture? How do you grow when what is planted and starts to grow is pulled up from the root every week?

If resurrection of the dead, healing, deliverance, consecration... are all elementary foundational works that we should have down (Hebrews 6:1-2)... and Jesus said you will do as I have done and greater works than these (John 14:12), wow... what lies beyond? Well, I know, this... I can't wait to go DEEPER IN GOD!! I am not a pew squatter... BRING IT ON DADDY GOD!!

When we are indeed crucified with Christ and dead to ourselves with Christ living in and through us, then ministry just happens. It's not a magic wand with a switch we can turn on and off. It's Jesus. There is a point of ignition found in intimate relationship between Bride and Bridegroom, Jesus and the church.

Your eternal destination isn't all that it's about. It's also about the free gift of it, being poured out of you and getting all over everyone you come in contact with. If this is new to you... well... you're about to have so much fun...

Falling in love with Jesus will knock the hell out of people... literally.

Trials, circumstances, our past... don't determine who we are. Our relationship with Christ does. When we burn for Him, what was is burned up and new life is conceived, in resurrection power.

Sit in a pew and keep your distance and He will be distant from you and wait patiently. He doesn't force Himself on us. He is a gentleman... most of the time. He waits and the Spirit woos us, draws us to Himself. He is our Lover. He does invade our lives sometimes, though. His longing is intimacy with us.

Be sure to bring God with you when you go soul-fishing... that is, if you want to catch anything. Fish are drawn to Light. Is He in you?

When a mother eagle knows her eaglets are ready to leave the nest and go make a home of their own, she turns the sticks upward so the nest is no longer a place of comfort. Christianity is like that... its hands on. We can give to the pastor, to the travelling evangelist and share in their fruit. But at some point, God will break our hearts for the lost, and that pew is going to feel real uncomfortable.

When I'm soul-fishing, I'm not standing on the edge of the sea, line in the water, thinking about last night's baseball scores. I am praying, asking God to show me who might be open to receive Jesus, asking God what to say... asking Him to make me His voice to lost souls... to release the prophetic in me to speak into people's lives to edify them... bring them to an intimate relationship with Daddy God... into the Kingdom for God's Glory. This is called bearing fruit to our Lover, Jesus, in Kingdom Culture Life.

Notice, there's no mention of sitting on a pew inside the four walls of a fellowship building preaching to the choir, trying to reproduce with other family members of the church. I will spare your ears and not use the "I" word in this statement. Point is, we need to do the "Jesus", and go soul-fishing.

Does Mark 16:15 say "Go ye into all the churches and preach the Gospel to every saved creature? Or does it say "Go ye into all the world and preach the Gospel to every creature (soul)?

Yes, let's come together for a celebratory service. Then get out. Yes, I said, "get out". We're at war here. Hey, I'm talking to me too. We don't need donuts and coffee. There are wounded, hurting, lost and dying souls needing what we have been equipped with...

Tasting of the Bread of Life is for our edification, the nurturing of our Spirit, to raise us up as warriors in Christ... to help make us His hands and feet, His voice... with wisdom and truth written on the tablets of our hearts. This brings maturation and fruit-bearing ability.

"Go ye into all the world and preach the Gospel"... Notice in that scripture, there's no mention of being a captive audience, but taking an interactive role. What is God saying and doing in and through you? Hey, I'm asking myself, too...

There's nothing comfortable about moving out of our pews, out of the four walls of the fellowship building (notice I didn't say "church"). This is where the story of our great adventure in Christ truly begins... to do as Christ did and greater things (John 14:12).

What possesses us pours out of our hearts. When we are possessed by God, He has consumed all that we are. We can only pour out all of His Holiness, all of His goodness. When we see something else, it is our old nature trying to resurrect itself. Break out your cross and seek your lover, your saviour, Jesus.

When the valley is deep, and the way out is long... will our lips still speak of the sweetness of the Lord? Will He still hear our love song in the midst of our suffering, our longing for Him? He is Lord of the valley, and Lord of the mountaintop. Even when we question, His heart always beats for us.

The man with HIV... the woman with STD... the child parenting a child... the elderly in need... the disabled, with nowhere to turn... the wounded warrior who gave his life, his children grieve. Yet tears of sorrow will turn to tears of joy, at the day of the Lord, the day of Glory. Until then, He kisses every tear.

What can religiosity do for the hurting heart... the empty soul longing to be filled, longing to be free? What can it do for the afflicted in need of healing... the one who's hunger and thirst never ends... except that they find Christ? Nothing of this world can fulfil this need. Religion offers illuminated moonlight, but still resides in darkness. So the question is this... will we be Jesus to them?

The world's way can teach them how to cope... to live in their need. But the Man from Galilee, He shows us how to overcome... and walk in the abundance of heaven on earth, if we'll only believe.

Mountains will move... chains will break... hope is found in the life of Christ in us, the hope of glory.

Will we be Jesus? Will we be Jesus to these? See their need... hear the cry of their hearts... God hears too... that's why He is sending us as His ambassadors of hope, with Christ, living and reigning in us...

Light a fire down in my soul, ignite the flame, 'cause I want more. All that is me, let it burn, but what is engraved, Your precious Word... all that is You, let it remain... covered in Your Love, and it's Crimson Stain.

What is "radical love"? See the man from Galilee, His arms of Love nailed to the cross. Willingly He poured Himself out... arms open wide, to show us the Love of the Father. Run to Him... run and don't look back... run and don't stop until His heart meets yours.

Afflictions of this life can either draw you into sin through taking offense... or you will be drawn to perfect love from the throne of God by a work of forgiveness... and victim and offender see the mountain move in both your lives... and both are changed forever.

Your ministry day begins the moment you love on somebody. A simple smile, a "God bless you", an "I love you"... We have no idea who's life out there may have been saved. I can't tell you how many times God has drawn me to someone for ministry, and after the tears flow and the Spirit moves and the healing hand of the Master touches their soul... they will then confess and share about the suicide letter they had just written before God led me to contact them... or some other tragic decision was in the balance in their time of desperation. THAT is God at work.

There is a place... at some point... where self gratification doesn't cut it anymore. It's that way with anything of this world we use to try to fill the great big abyss, the void in our heart that we are born with from separation from God at the garden. And nothing... I say NOTHING, will fill it or satisfy... but Jesus. Go ahead, keep trying... He will be there waiting patiently when you come to the end of yourself... with love in His eyes and mercy in His heart for you.

There is a parting going on... religiosity from the awakened and ignited (Matthew 10:34-35)... goats from the sheep. Look and see for yourself. It is the finger of God that moves them.

Honestly, sometimes we have to pray some people will lose themselves so they can be found. We pray that they reach the bottom of the barrel so they will look up in their desperation to find the face of Almighty God. It's in that place that they can only look up... and there He is, the God of this universe, their Creator, to meet them in their time of need... to offer restoration, renewal and resurrection life.

Jesus causes me to change my thinking of what a man should be in this world, in order to release heaven on earth. After all, are we not to be Christ like in this life, our carnal selves crucified with Christ that Jesus would live and reign in and through us? Jesus showed us, as a man, the example of the true human potential, sinless and Sprit-filled, by only doing what He saw the Father do and saying what He heard the Father say. There's no Todd in that equation. I am taking note of that..

When we pray and someone is healed, take a moment and think of the 39 stripes that paid for that healing... takes my breath away...

I can either crucify my carnal mind and have the mind of Christ... or I can crucify my carnal mind and have the mind of Christ. Yep, you're right... I only have one choice. It's either that or burn, baby burn... and I don't smoke.

If you're not living a heaven on earth life... well... you're missing out. Hey, I'm not there all the time, but I've had a taste of heaven. Take one guess where my ship is headed...

We can't let what we see cancel out what we believe will be. There's nothing impossible to those who believe... nothing.

I'm just here in humble amazement that I'm still alive, by His grace, and that He would find me worthy to be a vessel to work through, such a wretched man I was. In some ways, I still have some Todd to crucify too, ...because it resurrects itself from time to time. So God sits me down on his knee, pulls out his pocket knife and whittles away, just like my grandpa used to do to pieces of wood while sitting on his rocking chair on his porch w...hen I was a child. Yes, the Lord peels away the layers of yucky Todd, and makes me a fountain of Jesus once again. Beauty for ashes is an understatement.

Jesus could come take me home right now and I'd be ok with that. I've lived a long, hard, full life to this point. Heaven sounds like a wonderful place. Yet there is more life in me right now than ever before... new songs, new paintings, new nature scenes of wonder to travel to for photographing, new writings and teachings. How can this be? Am I the Eveready bunny? And yet when I see my elementary aged grandkids, they beat me in every computer game there is. Let me just be honest, they can outlast me in most things, period. How does that work exactly? God help me, there is a great big harvest field out there calling the name of the One who lives in me. There is so much to live for that I literally can't wait for my next breath. The sun is up... check... eyes open... check... pulse... check... coffee... check... more coffee... check... coffee IV ... don't even think about it!!... another day, new mercies... check... ok, Lord, let's get it on!!

God, but she said this about me, he said that... "Todd, they ripped his beard from His face and spat upon Him"... but God, they lied about me and said this and that... "they lashed Him with a cat o' nine tails and ripped His flesh from His very body"... but God, You know how Christians are and how that could effect my ministry... "then they nailed Him to a tree until He passed away, before My very eyes"... but, Father... "that should have been you up there on that cross... He took your place even though He was completely innocent, because He loves you that much"... Lord, forgive me... take my bitter, resentful, judgmental heart from me and restore me, renew me, whatever it takes, whatever the cost. I want nothing flowing from me but You... help me to forgive these and show them nothing but Jesus, even as they cast their stones...

We have to realize everything that is, is actually God's... then we don't get offended with others when they spitefully or inappropriately use or abuse us. What they do they do to Him. He will deal with their hearts. We don't have to. We just have to deal with ours. After all, is what we do for the glory of God or for our own boasting.

Joy fills our heart when our passion for God is ablaze. When the flame wanes, we slip into religion, where apathy and contentment greet us at the door. We keep the fire of passion burning with restless pursuit of a King who wrote our name in the Book of Life with His Blood.

There was a sudden case of stupid in the Intelligence Department in Washington D.C. the day "politically correct" was brought into consideration for national legislation.

Fear is the oil and match the enemy needs to burn away your hope... seek perfect love and watch few run... run as fast as it can.

Pursuing grace to receive all that it brings, without understanding the price that was paid to attain it, the love behind it... or experiencing the person of the One who paid that price... is like the bride who knows all about her Bridegroom, but never consummates the marriage.

Religion is like an eagle in a chicken coop. The knowledge is there, but there's no experience of the Kingdom... and the eagle remains unknown by the Lord.

When you see the Fire of God up ahead, what will you do but run toward it? ... because you know when you arrive, you will walk in a greater presence than ever before.

Here I am, Lord, once again... standing in the fire... but I don't feel the burn... I don't smell like smoke... and my heart is more alive than ever... must be Jesus is in the room...

Our identity is found in this alone... Christ... the lover of our soul... voluntarily took our place on the cross, spread His arms open wide, placed his feet at the bottom of the cross as they nailed Him to the tree... and with His public display of affection and love for us, expressed our value, our worth before God and man, with all the love He had in His heart. As a man, He cried out to God for us that we might spend eternity with the Father. Surely, we are precious in His sight.

Jesus came to restore humanity and all it's brokenness. This is the point where we release, from the life of Christ in us, heaven on earth... life as it was always meant to be.

The resurrection of Christ was the forerunner of our own destiny, (for He too came as a man): life eternal. He is the bridge, we need only to cross it, and step into the garden.

Works does not, cannot, and will not ever, replace intimate relationship and fellowship with God... no matter how hard we try. Does He know you?

We can manage our time. We can manage the space around us. We cannot manage our hearts. We need intimacy with God like we need the air we breathe.

Our passion, our dreams, our fears... all that we are... all that we are going to be... and the mysteries within the DNA that makes us who we are... cannot be controlled by principles alone. Our heart beats of it's own, by a power much greater than any we understand. Our hearts are moved by light and dark. In the light, we find the very source of all life... Creator to creation. Yes, there is a God, yes He loves us. Yes, He wants to be One with us. It's a beauty beyond compare.

Through adversity and great triumph... mountain peaks and deep valleys... the Spirit of the Living God draws you to Himself. Just listen to the wind, and catch it. Hold it, taste, smell the beautiful fragrance of it. It is Heaven that invades your spiritual atmosphere...

In our search for completeness, trying to fill the void we are born with that came from separation from our Creator in the garden... we walk through this life with this deep yearning desire for meaning, to satisfy the longing... a longing only restoration of intimate fellowship with the Creator, the One True Living God, can restore. In our pursuit we so often find that He was in our midst all along. It was us who lost ourselves... distracted with the things of this world. But God is patient, waiting for us to step out of the maze we call our lives... and we find wholeness in all He is.

We can run, we can hide. But there we are still. And such is this war we are born into, for our souls. Denying it and avoiding it won't make it go away. In fact, it allows the enemy to stay and do his bidding. We were afforded a full suite of armour for a reason.

Why? To know us... to love us and enjoy fellowship with us forever... Why? To know God... to love Him and enjoy fellowship with Him forever...

God desires an intimate relationship with us that is far more than anything we call intimacy here on earth... even intimate relations between husband and wife. There is a place in God some do not know of... a place in His heart that He is aching within Himself to take us, to walk with us, to reveal to us... if we are willing... if we can take our eyes off of ourselves and this earthly journey dimension long enough to step into our spiritual journey dimension.

When we surrender in an area, God's perfect love comes rushing in, and an overwhelming desire to have victory overwhelms fear. Resurrection power then brings renewed life and takes form with a deposit of heaven established in its place.

As our journey, the race, the good fight... grows long and sometimes treacherous, and war does rage on... we can be tempted to look for an easier way. But most often this only prolongs the journey with detours and distractions. The path is before us and we must finish the race... and we WILL see God.

The desire of our hearts is what lies under our hood. It makes us go. We are constantly looking for... striving to be... looking to do... longing for... to meet those desires. It is not unlike the passion we are born with having been born into a life with a hole in our hearts... a void... from being separated from God in the garden. There is always that seeking... it is a part of who we are. It drives us right to our destiny in this life on earth... and to the very face of God and all His glory.

Proof

Made in the USA
Charleston, SC
25 March 2014